To Lily Grace —

Happy 1st Christmas

Love from,

"Uncle" Tristan

x

My Very First
Bible Stories

Published by Candle Books
an imprint of
Lion Hudson plc
Wilkinson House, Jordan Hill Road,
Oxford OX2 8DR, England
www.lionhudson.com/candle

ISBN 978 1 78128 232 8
e-ISBN 978 1 78128 237 3

First edition 2015

A catalogue record for this book is available from the British Library

Printed and bound in Malaysia, July 2015, LH45

My Very First
Bible Stories

Retold by Juliet David

Illustrated by Pauline Siewert

**CANDLE
BOOKS**

Noah and his Great Ark

A great flood covers all the earth.
But Noah and his family
are safe inside the ark.
They have taken with them
two of every kind of animal.

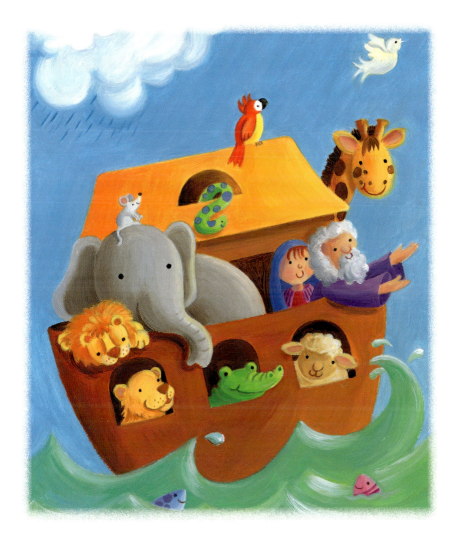

The rain stops.
The floods vanish.
Noah, his family, and all the
animals come out of the ark.
God puts a beautiful rainbow
high in the sky.

You can read this story in your Bible
in the book of Genesis chapters 6–9.

Moses and the Great Escape

Moses is leading his people out of Egypt.
They are trying to find a new land.
They reach the shores of the Red Sea
– but Egyptian soldiers
are chasing them.
How can they escape?

God opens a pathway across the sea.
Moses and all his people
walk safely across.
Then God closes up the water again.
Now the Egyptians
will never catch God's people!

You can read this story in your Bible in Exodus chapter 14.

David and the Giant Bully

David is a very small shepherd boy.
Goliath is a GIGANTIC soldier.
David has a shepherd's sling.
Goliath has a sword,
a shield, and a helmet.
Can David win the fight?

David chooses one stone
and hurls it with his sling.
The stone hits Goliath.
The giant drops down dead.
With God's help,
David defeats the horrible giant.

*You can read this story in your Bible in
1 Samuel chapter 17.*

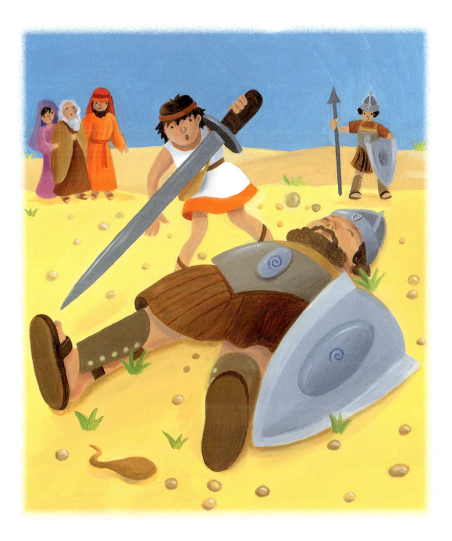

The Fish That Broke the Net

Simon and his friends
have been fishing all night.
Have they caught any fish?
No!
Not a single one.
What can they do?

"Sail out to deeper water!" says Jesus.
"Then let down your nets again."
Now the friends catch so many fish
that their nets begin to break.
"Lord Jesus," says Simon.
"You've done a great miracle!"

*You can read this story in your Bible
in Luke chapter 5 verses 1–11.*

A Very Happy Family

Jairus's little girl is very ill.
"Jesus," says Jairus.
"Please come and make her well."
But the little girl dies.
What can Jesus do now?

"Little girl, get up!" says Jesus.
At once she opens her eyes
and sits up in bed.
"Now bring her food," says Jesus.
What a wonderful miracle!

You can read this story in Luke chapter 8
verses 40–42 and 49–56.

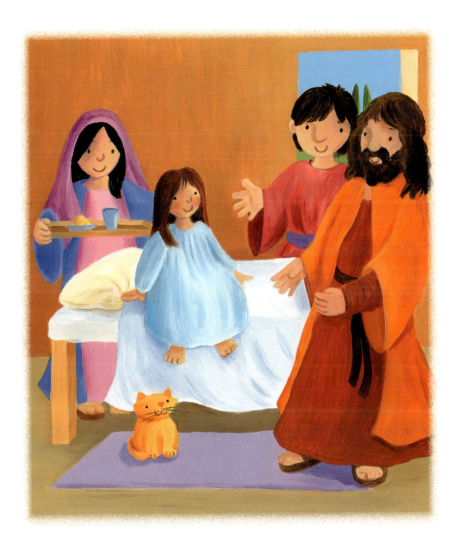

The Little Man in a Big Tree

Jesus is visiting town.
Everybody wants to see him.
Zacchaeus is very small
so he climbs a tall tree to watch.
Jesus stops under his tree and looks up.
What does he say to Zacchaeus?

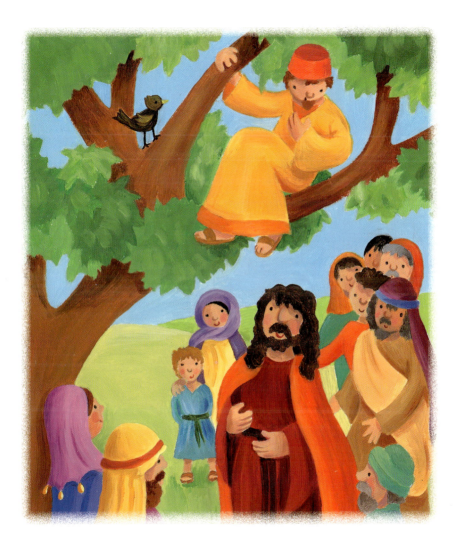

"Zacchaeus, come down," says Jesus.
"I want to eat at your house!"
Zacchaeus slides down the tree
and takes Jesus home.
After he meets Jesus,
Zacchaeus is a much better person.

You can read this story in Luke chapter 19 verses 1–9.